XAVIER HUDSON

SECRETS OF CLOSING THE SALE

The Ultimate Guide on How To Perfectly Close a Sale, Discover Effective Closing Techniques and Secrets That Would Make You a Successful Closer

Descrierea CIP a Bibliotecii Naţionale a României
XAVIER HUDSON
  SECRETS OF CLOSING THE SALE. The Ultimate Guide
on How To Perfectly Close a Sale, Discover Effective Closing
Techniques and Secrets That Would Make You a Successful
Closer / Xavier Hudson – Bucharest: Editura My Ebook, 2021
  ISBN

XAVIER HUDSON

SECRETS OF CLOSING THE SALE

The Ultimate Guide on How To Perfectly Close a Sale, Discover Effective Closing Techniques and Secrets That Would Make You a Successful Closer

My Ebook Publishing House
Bucharest, 2021

TABLE OF CONTENTS

INTRODUCTION

The closer is the king of the business world. If he played baseball, he'd be the powerhouse home run hitter. If he was a golfer, he'd have a scratch handicap with the smoothest touch on any green in the world. He's that heavyweight boxer who knows when to float like a butterfly and when to sting like a bee. He's a pro who knows all the angles and who's seen it all. He's the main man, the go-to guy and the ringer all in one. Why? The answer is simple. The closer makes money.

Money is what sales is all about. Think about that for a second. It's one of those blatantly obvious thoughts that, upon consideration, become deceptively complex. A great many people make the mistake in assuming that sales is about technique or presentation or product knowledge. While successful salesmanship does, in part, touch upon all those things, it is not about any them. Instead, a sale is about money, nothing more and nothing less. Anyone who thinks differently is being, intentionally or unintentionally, naive.

A successful salesperson understands that their job is to generate income by convincing a customer to purchase what they are offering for sale. Moreover, they also understand that their job is to convince that customer that what they're selling is vastly superior to what the competition is selling. Finally, and perhaps most importantly, they understand that their job is to make the customer want and need to possess the product or service they're selling more than anything else. Part drill instructor, part psychologist and part succubus, the closer is like no else in the business world.

As the title suggests, this book is about learning the most innovative, as well as the most effective, ways to close a sale. Good sales techniques equal good sales. Good sales equal a healthy bottom line for everyone involved. However, before we get to the specifics of the art of closing the sale, let's take a look at a couple of the primary concepts that quality closing depends upon.

Closing - What Is It?

Closing, at its most basic, is successfully selling something to someone. However, it's extremely important at the outset to understand that simply selling for the sake of the sale is a mistake. No matter how important sales are to a particular business (and they ARE extremely important), no sales momentum can be maintained by shoving product out the door and down customer's throats.

Every actual or potential salesperson has seen the 1992 film of the David Mamet play *Glengarry Glen Ross*. The play follows four salesmen in a Chicago real estate office over the course of two days. An outside sales trainer is sent to the office to increase profits through a sales contest where the top two performers will be rewarded with lucrative "warm" leads and the bottom two will be terminated. In his opening speech to the salesmen, the trainer tells them, "A-B-C. A-Always, B-Be, C-Closing. Always be closing, always be closing."

While entertaining, the sales philosophy in *Glengarry Glen Ross* is antiquated. High pressure, high stakes, sales pitches fall flat when it comes to consumers who have come to expect more from the businesses they deal with. Smart salespeople know that while closing a sale is the reason they're there, more has to go into the process than the end result.

Successful closing is more like a dialogue between two people with different, yet similar, needs than it is a monologue delivered by a hard sell go getter. The salesperson and the customer engage in this dialogue to fulfill these needs. The customer has a need that they want met. The salesperson has a product or a service that fills that need. Throughout the dialogue, both parties exchange information that helps them explore mutual opportunities while establishing mutual trust.

In this scenario, the close itself is the valediction in a long conversation. At the point it happens, it is both inevitable and expected by both parties. From the needs of the salesperson and the customer flows an informational exchange that results in mutual satisfaction. So instead of ABC, always be closing, a good closer prefers to say CAN, closing as needed.

The Importance of Lead Generation to Closing

Every party to a sales transaction is important, but none more so than the lead. Without leads there are no prospects, without prospects there are no sales and without sales there is no business. The best closer in the world cannot operate in a vacuum. If there are no potential customers, then there is no dialogue that will lead to the closing of a sale.

Leads are generated in a number of ways that can be separated into two broad groups - outbound leads and inbound leads. Both groups have their place in the world of sales, as well as their prospective proponents. However, a good closer knows the difference between the two, as well as how to successfully approach each one given the circumstances.

Outbound leads are generated through outbound marketing. Outbound marketing mainly consists of television, radio and print advertising. A business advertises its products and/or services to a certain demographic and hopes that these ads will generate sufficient potential customers to insure a healthy bottom line. Outbound leads tend to be "warm", in that they found something attractive in the advertising that relates to a need.

Inbound leads are generated through inbound marketing. As the name implies, inbound marketing is the opposite of outbound marketing. With outbound marketing, a business will create content regarding its products, services, business history or even business philosophy. This content will then be used to attract the attention of interested parties who will provide contact information in exchange for the content. This contact information will then be used to generate a greater and greater involvement of the customer with the products and/or services being offered for sale. Inbound leads tend to be "warmer" than outbound leads due to this preexisting level of involvement and exchange.

The main difference between inbound and outbound lead generation lies in how they approach the pool of potential leads they are addressing. Outbound generation attempts to forcefully grab a share of these potential leads by appealing to a need or desire that may exist within the group. Inbound generation, on the other hand, attempts to attract specific individuals who may already be searching for ways to satisfy a desire or need. It lets this market segment develop a trust in the product or service before segueing into the closing dialogue.

Sales Approaches and How They Relate to Closing

Throughout history there has been any number of approaches developed with an eye to making a sale. These approaches vary with time, culture and product. However, an overall understanding of what they are and how they relate to closing a sale can help anyone become a better salesperson.

The hard sell is an approach that is familiar to almost everyone because everyone, at one time or another has been on the receiving end of this approach. The hard sell depends on being able to strong arm the customer into a purchase through intimidation and fear. Intimidation is used to make the customer appear weak or foolish if they fail to move on what is on offer. Fear is used to motivate the customer to purchase lest the offer for sale be removed. Either way, the hard sell is what gives sales, as a profession, a bad name. Because of this it has, largely, fallen into disfavor.

The soft sell is an approach that is the exact opposite of the hard sell. Instead of strong arming the customer, the soft sell attempts to use suggestion and helpfulness as a means to convince the customer to buy. In the right hands, and with the right product, the soft sell can be a very effective sales approach. If a customer is already in the right mental space, a hint or tip or even a bit of behind the scenes information is all that's needed to bring the sale to a close. However, in the wrong hands, or if it is overused, the soft sell can come across as smarmy and fawning and have the opposite of its intended effect.

Selling against the competition is perhaps the oldest of all sales approaches. There's an old sales story about two men who are out in the woods when they startle a bear and her cubs. As the angry mother bear charges, the two men begin to run away. As they are running, one man yells "We can't outrun a bear, we're doomed!" The other man yells back "I don't have to outrun a bear, I only have to outrun you!" Nothing could illustrate the concept of selling against the competition better. If two retailers sell the same product and one retailer offers that product at a given price, all the other has to do in order to sell against his competitor is to offer the product at a lower price.

Selling on value is an especially important approach for the would-be closer to pay attention to. In essence, selling on value is the opposite of selling against the competition. When you sell against the competition you rely on your lower price when compared to theirs. When you sell on value, you justify a potentially higher price tag by emphasizing the benefits that will accrue to the buyer despite the price. Highlighting these benefits serves the dual purpose of making the competition's product looking shoddy while making yours seem well worth the extra cost. The fact that the buyer gets a positive feeling for making a wise, yet difficult choice often can seal the deal.

Value added selling is exactly what it the name implies - the salesperson sweetens the pot in order to close the sale. This additional value, at no additional cost, often persuades the customer to pull the trigger on the sale. This added value can be almost anything - additional features, a newer or more advanced model or an extended warranty of guarantee. It can also take the form of added benefits to the customer; such as at home set up or free delivery. The point is that the added value is leverage to close the sale at no real extra cost to the salesperson or the business. These costs were prefigured into the sales price and are only added as leverage if necessary.

Branding for reputation is an excellent approach to increasing sales. Branding relies on the customer to recognize the quality of a given product or service based on previous experience or on word of mouth from other satisfied customers. It also relies on the perception of the brand among consumers who have no prior experience with the product or service or who have no second hand knowledge of the same. There are many high end or high tech products that use this approach very successfully. A certain computer/phone/handheld device company named after a fruit is an excellent example of branding for reputation.

Now that we've taken a look at some of the primary concepts involved in developing an understanding of various sales approaches, it's time to dive into the specifics of innovative sales closing. These powerful methods have been proven to generate a high percentage of successful closes, the type of closes your business needs to have in order to stay in the business of generating profit. Let's get started.

THE ANATOMY OF A CLOSER

So, what does a closer look like? Is a closer a slick looking guy or girl with too much hair product and a history of orthodontics? Is a closer a no nonsense professional in a well-tailored suit with a take no prisoners' aWtude? Is a closer a techno-geek that knows more about a particular line of products than the engineers who designed them? The answer is both yes and no.

A closer is someone who knows their customers better than the customers know themselves. A closer is well informed and well prepared for any and all eventualities that might occur during the selling process. A closer looks the part, well dressed and well groomed, because he or she lives the part. Yet, a closer can be, literally, the average guy or girl next door.

That's because the most successful salespeople have internalized the methods necessary to sell anything to anyone at any time. The proper approaches to a sale have become second nature to them. They walk the walk and potential customers sense this. In order to understand these methods and how they work, let's take a closer look at the anatomy, if you will, of the average closer.

Motivation

One of the most common characteristics among closers is motivation. Of course, it goes without saying that they are highly motivated to successfully complete a sale with a potential customer. Yet, what most people don't realize is that this motivation extends to other areas in their lives as well. A closer is driven to excel at nearly everything they attempt to accomplish. Excellence is the passion that fires their drive.

This is a trait they share with other highly motivated individuals outside the world of sales. Like a professional athlete, they are compelled to be the very best they can be. They want to succeed more than they want to eat, sleep or even breathe. This determination and focus on a goal is what sets them apart from the average salesperson. When failure is not an option you will consider, then you've taken the first step towards becoming a closer yourself.

Belief

If you don't believe in yourself, or in what you are doing, you can never achieve success. The closer understands this and this understanding, in turn, has an influence on their outlook, both internally and externally.

Weakness and uncertainty are directly correlated to failure. If you are consistently failing to achieve a measure of success and happiness in your life, it is probably due to the lack of belief you have in yourself and your abilities. This lack of belief not only affects you professional life, it drags you down personally as well. Clients smell that you lack confidence like an animal smells fear. Friends, relations, spouses and significant others sense it too.

The successful salesperson has worked hard to hone their abilities. They have acquired the knowledge they need to confidently perform their job to the best of their abilities. This knowledge has also allowed them to completely understand the product and service they are selling to their customers. They know that what they sell is the best choice for their clients. The clients see this confidence and it rubs off. They trust the closer and, through him or her, they trust in the quality of what they are being sold. In this way, belief becomes the glue that cements the sale.

Sincerity

Human beings are creatures of habit. We learn from past experiences and use the memories of those experiences to make judgments about current situations. This kind of behavioral learning helps to keep people alive by stopping them from making the same mistakes over and over. We learn to avoid situations that are similar to those that caused harm in the past. Likewise, we learn to trust situations that have resulted in positive outcomes.

We not only judge situations, we also judge people. We have learned to read dozens upon dozens of verbal and non-verbal cues in the first few minutes we interact with someone new. This unconscious pigeonholing helps us avoid harmful or unpleasant people and gravitate towards people who may be helpful or beneficial.

A competent salesperson understands the psychology behind this behavior and works with it in order to establish trust with his or her customers. This is done by talking in a conversational tone, keeping a calm demeanor and projecting a sincere desire to help the customer come to a satisfactory resolution to the problem they are facing. Taking these steps allows the salesperson to establish a rapport with the customer and this rapport is what helps that salesperson close the deal.

Focus

In order to sell something to someone you have to know what it is that they want. How do determine what they want? You focus on their need to solve a problem and not on your need to close a sale. It is this attention to the customer that helps the successful closer rack up sale after sale in a seemingly effortless manner.

Every customer comes into a selling situation with a particular need or problem. They are there specifically because of that need or problem. They actually want the salesperson to solve their problem or meet their need by selling them a solution. All the salesperson has to do to make the sale is find the best way to do what the customer already wants done.

A closer accomplishes this by asking the customer questions. The answers to these questions provide the closer with the information he or she needs to solve the problem the customer has presented them with. It only a matter of listening to what the customer has to say. They are the ones providing the closer with the information needed to seal the deal. If you focus on the customer, instead of yourself, you will greatly increase your chances of making the sale.

Takeaways for This Section

- Closers are defined by their methods, as well as their outlook;

- Closers internalize these methods and approach each sale in a positive frame of mind;

- Closing is not a 9 to 5 job, it is a way of life;

- Closers are highly motivated individuals who are in the game to won the game;

- Closers are confident in their abilities and believe in themselves and the solutions they sell;

- Closers understand that trust is the most important aspect of selling. They use their understanding of human psychology to establish this trust in a sincere and genuine manner;

- Closers focus on the customer's needs and wants, not on their need to make a sale.

THE SET UP

Steps to Take Before a Close

Preparation in sales, as in life, is everything. Often the individual who is most prepared is the individual that succeeds. A closer understands that laying the groundwork is crucial in every sales situation. Because forewarned is forearmed, a closer does their homework well ahead of a scheduled sales call. They are fully prepared BEFORE they enter the door for a sales meeting. Because of the importance of preparation in successful selling, this section will take a close look at some of the steps that are necessary to set up a close.

Closing a Sale Starts at the Beginning

We've all heard the old saying "If you want to make an omelet, you have to break some eggs". The point the saying is trying to make is that in order make a good omelet you have to take the necessary steps in preparation. Well, the same principle applies to sales. If you want to successfully close a sale, you have to prepare for the moment of closing ahead of time.

A closer starts his or her day ready to sell. They know that the actual close is simply the last act in a long and well thought out campaign. They understand that selling is much more than an exchange of money for goods or services. The more the closer knows about his prospects and their needs, the more he or she can use this knowledge to the best advantage. Know your customers. Know your products and services. If your actions well before the sale process are designed for success then the outcome of your sales call is foregone conclusion.

Dress for the Part You Want to Play

This one is simple and straightforward. Clothes actually do make the man or the woman. How you look and how you dress send the clearest and loudest message to everyone around you. You want to make sure that this message is the one you intend to send.

Human beings are visual creatures. We make snap judgments all the time based upon what we see or think we see. These snap judgments mean that your potential customers will have decided who you are and whether they like you in first three seconds that they see you. You will have one chance and one chance only to make a good impression. Don't blow that chance. Make sure you are appropriately dressed for success.

This doesn't mean expensive clothing, jewelry and accessories. It does mean neat, clean clothes that are appropriate for the environment. Jeans and a tee shirt are not going to cut it in a corporate meeting room, nor will they help you close a high dollar sale. Remember that you are playing the part of a professional facilitator who is worthy of a customer's trust and confidence. Dress to play that part.

Prospects and Planning

Before you can make a sale, you need to generate leads. If there are no leads (or no good leads), there will be no sales. Therefore, one of the most important steps to take in seWng up a successful close is prospecting for leads.

Leads come from everywhere. Of course they can come from marketing efforts, but they can also come from conversations at parties, watching the news and from just being prepared when the moment arises. Let's look at an excellent example of being prepared.

There's an apocryphal story in sales circles about a sales executive for a gardening company in North America that grew and sold, among other things, cacti and succulents. This executive was traveling and at his destination airport he found that there was a shortage of limousines and taxis. Therefore, he was forced to share a limo with three other business people for the drive into the city. During this drive the four people exchanged small talk and our executive discovered that one of the people sharing the limo with him was the main buyer for a major big box retailer.

The night before on the news, our salesman saw a report on how a hurricane had devastated Mexico's agricultural output, including its output of cacti and succulents. He also knew that the big box retailer imported the vast majority of the cacti and succulents for their stores from Mexico. Now, here he was, a cacti salesman, in the same limo as the guy from that retailer responsible for buying cacti!

When they reached the hotel where the buyer was staying, our salesman knew that it was go time. Ditching his own meeting, he followed the big box buyer into the hotel. When he saw the buyer heading for the men's room, he made his move. Stepping up to the urinal next to the buyer, he excused himself, explained who he was and made his elevator speech. (More on what that is in a minute.) He walked out of that men's room with the buyer's business card, a personal contact number and an appointment for a phone consultation. Two days later, he closed a twenty million dollar deal. The reason that deal occurred was because our salesman was prepared to follow a hot lead no matter when it showed up and no matter where it went - even into a bathroom.

The point of this story is to be prepared, even if there seems to be no need for the preparation. When you live and breathe for the products and services you sell, you're ready to close a deal on those products and services at a moment's notice or at the drop of a hat.

Greeting Prospects and Your Elevator Speech

Along with the way you dress, the way you speak and carry yourself helps create a good impression with your prospects. A lot of this stuff is a no brainer, but it bears repeating. If you have made an appointment, don't be late. Arrive for the appointment at least ten minutes ahead of time. This gives you an opportunity to relax for a moment and gather you thoughts. It also gives your prospect the same opportunity.

When you first greet your prospect, make direct eye contact and keep that contact while you introduce yourself. A firm and confident handshake is important. You don't need to try and crush your prospects hand, but you don't want to give them the impression that they are holding a dead fish either. Also, don't play any dominance games during your handshake by trying to keep your thumb in a higher position than your prospect or any other nonsense that you may have read. A quick, firm handshake accompanied by a simple introduction and eye contact. That's it.

This is a good time to discuss your elevator speech. An elevator speech is how you would describe yourself, your business and your philosophy if you only had fifteen seconds to do so. It's called an elevator speech, because it should be capable of being spoken on an elevator ride between stops.

Your speech needs to be more than who you are and what you do. It should be capable of encapsulating the essence of you are and what you do, as well as capture the attention of anyone hearing it. Think short, pithy and pointed, instead of long, boring and obvious.

For example, if you were selling insurance, telling people that you are in the business of taking a small amount of money from your customers and returning large amounts of money when they really need it. A lawyer might say that they are the last person you want to call when times are good and the first person you want to call when things go bad.

If your elevator speech is strong enough, you may find that you can generate leads simply by telling people what it is you do. That's the point. A closer impresses his or her prospects by simply walking in the room, shaking hands and telling the prospect who they are.

Listen and Learn

A lot of unsuccessful salespeople make the mistake of thinking that they are the stars of the sales process. They think the sale is all about them and what they have to say. Because their egos are bigger than their sales skills, they usually end up talking too much and listening too little. The result is that they scare off the prospect and lose the opportunity for a close.

As was said earlier, your prospect wants to buy from you. They want to believe in you. They want to trust you. They want you to make their life easier by solving their problem. All you, as a successful salesman, need to do is fulfill your end of the bargain by listening to what the prospect is telling you.

If the prospect is telling you about a specific problem they are having or about a specific goal they have in mind, address that problem or goal directly by offering them a solution. Do not, under any circumstances, ignore what they've said and talk about a solution to a problem they are not experiencing and couldn't care less about. They are telling you how to close the deal. All you have to do is listen to what they are saying, respond appropriately and the close is yours. In short, when you listen to your prospects, you learn how to successfully sell to them.

Takeaways for This Section

- A closer is prepared to close the sale before the sales pitch starts;

- Knowledge is power. A successful salesperson knows and understands what they are selling and who they are selling it to;

- A closer dresses for success. They dress appropriately for the situation because they know that they have only one chance to make a good impression;

- Sales come from leads and leads come from everywhere. A closer knows this and is prepared for any sales situation that may arise;

- How you carry yourself and how you speak are as important as how you are dressed when it comes to a good impression. A firm handshake, solid eye contact and a clever opening go a long way to guaranteeing a close;

Your prospect is telling you how to close the deal. A closer understands this and listens to his or her prospects to learn the best way to close.

HOW TO CLOSE

So far we covered a lot of essential background information that is necessary to laying the groundwork for a close. Now we are going to move on to the meat and potatoes and talk about the actual close itself. The process itself is deceptively simple. There are no secrets or tricks to doing it correctly. Despite this, there are an amazing number of salespeople who drop the ball right here on the goal line.

The essence of a successful close is knowing when to ask for the customer's business. Like asking someone out on a date or to get married, there is no "right" time. Instead, you have to plan your moves and feel out the situation before you pop the question. Your instincts have as much to do with the chances for success as anything else. An ill-timed close is about as uncomfortable for all involved as an unwanted marriage proposal.

Again, you have to do your homework. If you've laid the proper groundwork, knowing when to close is a breeze. The moment to do so will come naturally and inevitably as day following night. However, if you get lazy and you don't do your prep work the moment to close will never occur naturally or otherwise. You will have to try and force the close from an unwilling client. This forced action, more likely than not, will lead to a failure to close. So, let's take a quick look at those prep steps one more time.

First, focus on the prospect and their problem, not on you and your need for a sale. The sales process revolves around the customer. You, the salesperson are there for one reason and one reason only - to facilitate the solution to the customer's problem. That's your purpose. That's your role, nothing more and nothing less. If you solve the customer's problem, you close the sale.

Second, listen to your customer. If you listen to your customer, you get to know your customer. If you know your customer, you have the opportunity to develop a relationship with them. This relationship, in turn, leads to increased trust. Finally this trust increases the chance for a successful final act to the sale cycle.

Additionally, when you listen to your customer, you are learning both the nature of their problem and how they want you to solve that problem. These two pieces of information are critical to a successful close and your customer, more often than not, will hand them to you, but only if you shut up and listen.

Speaking of shuWng up, when it's time to close shut your mouth. Simply smile, ask for the customer's business as if it's a foregone conclusion and wait. Don't say another word. Far too many inexperienced salespeople have talked their way out of a close by failing to shut their mouths. You don't need to be giving the customer any further information at this point. If you've done your job and focused on and listened to the customer, you've already acknowledged their problem and offered a solution. Give them the opportunity to accept that offer.

Finally, once the customer agrees, seal the deal by forwarding any necessary paperwork promptly. Remember there is no deal until the ink is dry on the bottom line of any contract. Also, don't be afraid to ask for referrals from your customer. A satisfied and happy customer will be more than willing to give you referrals or recommend your services to colleagues. These referrals and recommendations can yield valuable new leads and we all know how important leads are to the sales process. Don't be afraid to ask.

Takeaways for This Section

- Timing is of the essence when it comes to a successful close. If you've done your job, your instincts will tell you when the moment is right to "pop the question";

- A salesperson is a facilitator and nothing more. A closer knows this and brings his or her focus to the customer and their problem, not onto their need for a sale;

  Listen to your customer and develop a relationship based on trust. This will pay dividends when it comes time to close;

- Listen to your customer some more. They will tell you their problem and how to solve that problem. Armed with that information, a closer is unstoppable;

- Smile, ask for the customer's business and shut up. If you've done your job, the outcome is guaranteed and needs no further help from you;

- Follow up after the close with any paperwork to legally seal the deal. Also ask for referrals and recommendations. They are an excellent source for new leads.

SALES MYTHS OR WHAT NOT TO DO

Now that you know pretty much everything you know to become a more successful closer, you need to take a look at a couple of sales mistakes. These are things that you should never do if you want to successfully close a deal. These are the mistakes that many unsuccessful people make time and time again. If you don't want to become the anti-closer, avoid these missteps like the plague.

Your Brochures and Website Don't Matter to the Customer

Sure you probably have all kinds of handouts and online information available for your customer to peruse. Don't mistake these materials for actual salesmanship. Anyone can read a brochure to a customer or direct them to a website. If the brochure or website was all the customer needed to purchase your product or service then you'd be extraneous. You are the bridge between the customer and what you are selling. The sales materials are there simply to generate leads and attract interest. You are the motive force when it comes to generating sales.

Make Sure That You're Talking to the Right Person

You put a lot of time and effort into making a sale. You got to know the customer, and established trust by focusing on them and not on you. You listened to the customer and noted their problem and how they'd like that problem solved. Now, when it comes time for the close, you belatedly realize that the person you've been dealing with for all this time is not the person who is able to make the final decision regarding the sale. Talk about wasted time and effort. Figure out who calls the shots when it comes to saying yes to your sales pitch ahead of time. You'll end up with a lot more money in your pocket and a lot less egg on your face.

A Hard Sell is Hard to Sell It's a big myth among the general public that sales is all about the hard sell. Heck, it's even a myth among salespeople who ought to know better. We've all got this stereotype stuck in our heads of the hard bitten, hard driving salesman making his own way among the wilds of the marketplace. He was successful, but now time, age and diminishing capacity are geWng the better of him. The problem is that this stereotype is just that - a myth. Hard bitten, hard driving sales are, and always have been, an anathema to the buying public.

No customer needs or wants to be bullied or humiliated into a purchase any more than they want to be bullied or humiliated into doing anything else. Bullying and humiliation are not attractive social behaviors and selling is a social business. Don't make the mistake of buying into a stereotype at the expense of your reputation and bottom line. A successful closer knows what it takes to get the job done.

Takeaways for This Section

- There are several sales misconceptions that a closer avoids at all cost;

- Sales materials are no substitute for skillful salesmanship;

- If you're not talking to the person who has the authority to make a sales decision then you're wasting time and effort. Do your homework and talk to the right person from the start of the sales process;

No one likes the hard sell. No one.

CONCLUSION

We've taken a look at some very effective methods used by proved closers to generate sales time after time, year after year. These methods are time tested and, if properly applied, work to bring every sales process to a successful conclusion. It isn't rocket science, but it does take work and planning to be effective. People want to be sold on a product or a service; they wouldn't be in the marketplace if they weren't in the market for something. The closer knows how to convert this desire to buy into a healthy bottom line. Now, you do too.

Printed by Libri Plureos GmbH in Hamburg,
Germany